GREAT PREDATORS

GREAT WHITE SHARK

by Nancy Furstinger

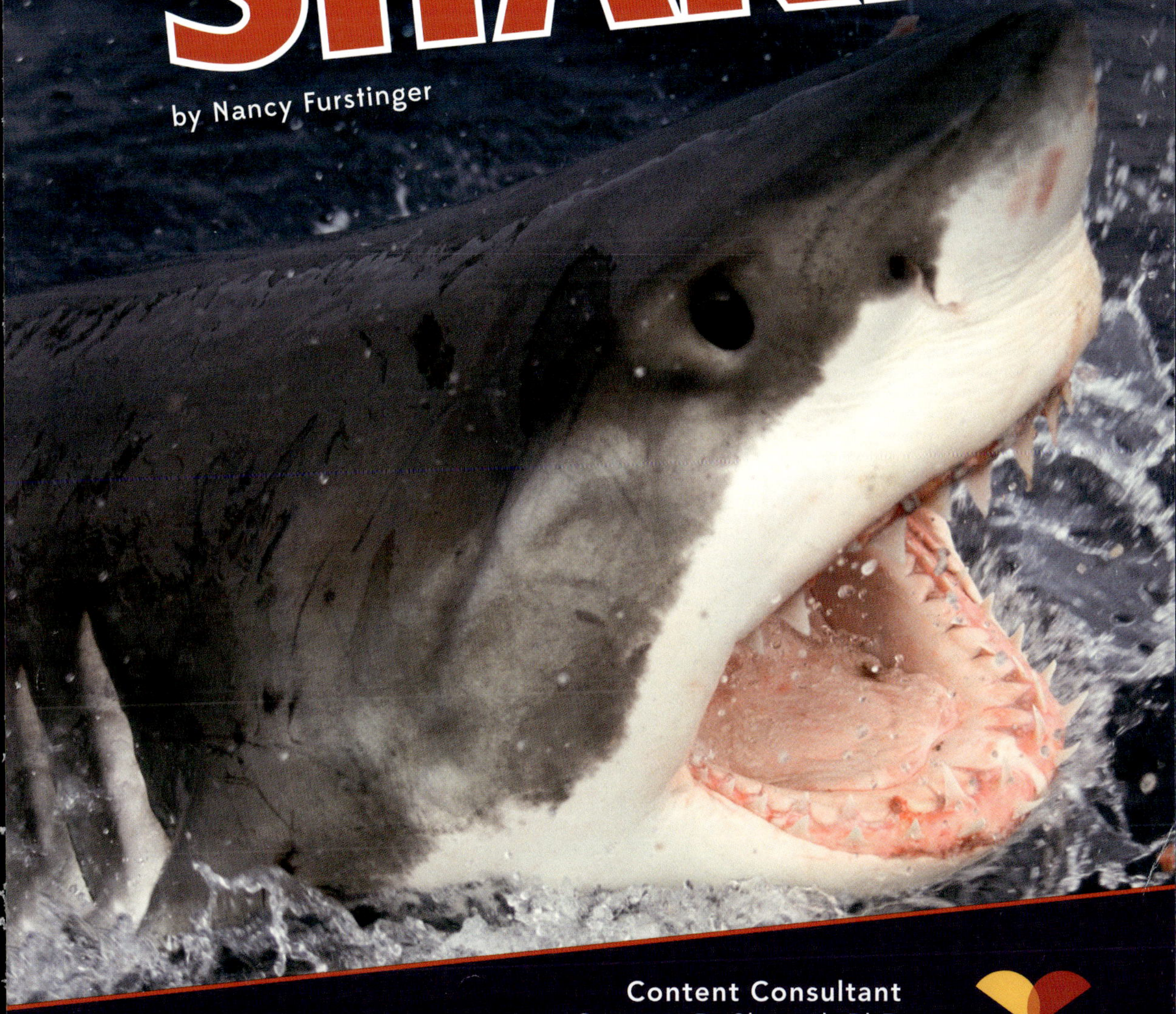

Content Consultant
Gregory B. Skomal, PhD
Marine Fisheries Scientist and Shark Specialist

CORE LIBRARY

Published by ABDO Publishing Company, PO Box 398166, Minneapolis, MN 55439.

Printed in the United States of America,
North Mankato, Minnesota
042013
092013
THIS BOOK CONTAINS AT LEAST 10% RECYCLED MATERIALS.

Editor: Lauren Coss
Series Designer: Becky Daum

Library of Congress Control Number: 2013932508

Cataloging-in-Publication Data
Furstinger, Nancy.
Great white shark / Nancy Furstinger.
p. cm. -- (Great Predators)
ISBN 978-1-61783-947-4 (lib. bdg.)
ISBN 978-1-62403-012-3 (pbk.)
Includes bibliographical references and index.
1. Great white sharks--Juvenile literature. 2. White sharks--Juvenile literature. 3. Sharks--Juvenile literature. 4. Predatory animals--Juvenile literature. I. Title.
597.3--dc23

2013932508

Photo Credits: Minden Pictures/SuperStock, cover, 1; Tony Hunt/Shutterstock Images, 4; Thinkstock, 6, 11, 22, 25, 26, 43; Shutterstock Images, 9; Stephen Frink/Science Faction/SuperStock, 12; MIVA Stock/SuperStock, 15; Everett Collection, 17; Minden Pictures/SuperStock, 18, 20; David P. Stephens/Shutterstock Images, 28; Red Line Editorial, 30; Stephan Savoia/AP Images, 32; Neil Bradfield/iStockphoto, 34; Kike Calvo/AP Images, 37; Kin Cheung/AP Images, 38; David Royal/Monterey County Herald/AP Images, 40, 45

CONTENTS

CHAPTER ONE

DEADLY JAWS

A lone harbor seal returns home after supper. The seal is tired and plump with squid. It surfaces from a kelp forest off the Southern California shoreline. Suddenly a sleek gray torpedo races beneath the seal. It's a great white shark. And it is launching a sneaky surprise attack! The huge hunter snatches the seal in one swift strike. Its deadly jaws snap the seal's neck. The shark shakes its prey from

Great white sharks are some of the deadliest predators in the ocean.

A great white shark's body is streamlined like a torpedo.

side to side, sawing the seal apart. Then the shark splashes down. It gobbles up the seal in three giant bites.

A Big, Hungry Fish

The great white shark is the largest predator in the ocean. This meat-eating fish can grow more than 20 feet (6 m) long. That's about the length of an African elephant. Great white sharks can weigh up to

5,000 pounds (2,268 kg). The great white shark's body is built for speed. This shape allows the shark to swim in bursts of speed up to 35 miles per hour (56 km/h).

Great white shark skeletons are made of cartilage. This is the same material that the tips of your nose and ears are made of. Cartilage is lightweight and flexible. This helps the shark swim efficiently. The shark uses its powerful tail to propel through water. A triangle-shaped dorsal fin on the shark's back gives it balance while swimming. A pair of pectoral fins look and act like airplane wings. These help the shark steer.

Skin Teeth

Sharkskin is covered with tiny teeth-like scales called denticles. These scales point toward the tail. They reduce friction. This helps the shark rapidly slide through the sea. If you were to stroke the sharkskin from head to tail, it would feel as smooth as rubber. However, if you were to stroke in the reverse direction, the skin would feel rough like sandpaper. These tiny scales also keep sharks clean. Barnacles and other sea creatures can't get a grip on sharkskin.

The shark's gray back blends in with the dark ocean below. This makes it difficult to spot the shark from above. The shark's white underbelly blends in with the water's sunlit surface when viewed from below. These two colors, called countershading, help camouflage the shark from its prey.

Electricity Detectors

Great white sharks' snouts contain tiny open pores. Within these pores are gel-filled cells that can detect electricity. All animals give off electric charges with each beat of their hearts and each contraction of their muscles. Sharks can sense the power and direction of these electrical fields. They use this special sense to help find prey nearby.

Super Senses

Super senses help great whites become top hunters. Two-thirds of a shark's brain is devoted to smell. Great whites can sniff out a single drop of blood floating in 10 billion drops of water.

Great whites also have sharp eyesight. They can spot prey in shadowy waters and at night. Sharks can even roll

Great whites use their teeth and powerful jaws to rip and tear bite-sized chunks out of their prey.

their eyes back into their sockets for protection during fights with seals and other prey.

Sharks' ears are tiny. But they are mighty. Great white sharks can sense sound vibrations in the water. This allows them to zero in on swimming and splashing prey.

Sharks also have a series of sense organs called lateral lines beneath their skin. The organs run in a

Great Whites Go Digital

You can study great white sharks in the wild alongside scientists with a new app called Shark Net. Shark Net allows users to connect with sharks in real time. When the sharks swim by underwater listening stations, signals are sent to a satellite. Then a free computer program sends instant data about shark sightings to the app user. The app also features 3D models of sharks, videos, and maps. Researchers hope the app will help raise awareness about sharks and their habitats.

line from the head to the tail down each side of the shark's body. They act as motion sensors. They detect changes in water pressure due to the movements of possible prey.

One of the great white shark's most effective predatory characteristics is its most famous one. A great white shark has approximately 300 sharp, serrated teeth. These teeth are arranged in up to seven rows. Young great whites have pointed teeth to grasp fish. As the sharks reach adulthood, their tooth shape changes. Adult shark teeth grow to approximately 2.5 inches (6.4 cm) long. Upper teeth

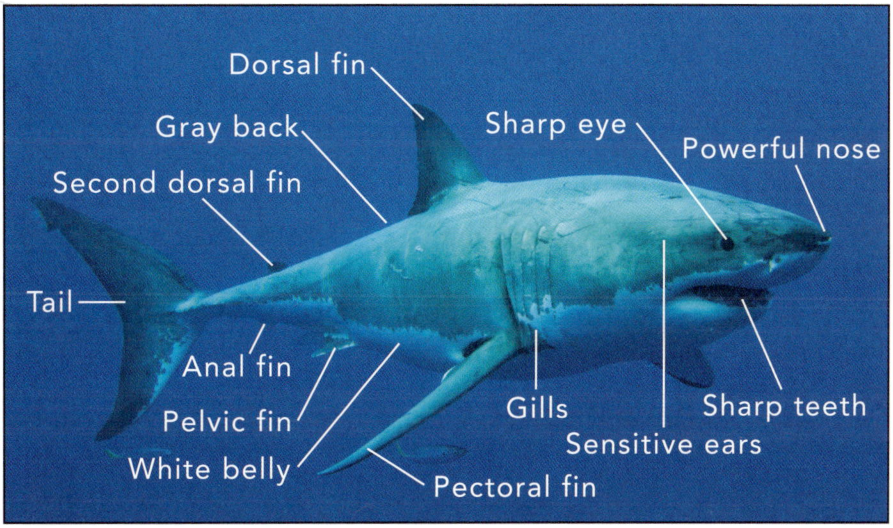

Great White Shark Predatory Features

Great white sharks have many special predatory characteristics that make them top hunters. This diagram shows where some of these features are located on a great white shark. How might these special characteristics make the great white a better hunter?

resemble saws. The lower teeth are narrower. These two shapes allow sharks to seize and gobble up prey, such as seals.

An adult great white shark may seem like a terrifying predator. But great white sharks need to be ready to defend themselves before they are even born. Only the strongest and toughest great white shark pups, or babies, will grow up to become top ocean predators.

CHAPTER TWO

A GREAT WHITE'S LIFE

Great white sharks spend most of their lives alone. However, males and females pair up during mating season. Most researchers think this probably takes place from April to September. Male sharks are ready to mate starting at about nine years of age. Females wait until they are about 14 years old. Great white sharks breed once every two years.

Great white sharks are usually solitary predators.

Baby Shark Food

After hatching inside the mother shark, the baby sharks gobble up any unfertilized eggs. Developing pups shed their teeth as they grow. The pups swallow teeth as they shed them. This provides the pups with calcium and other minerals.

No one has witnessed great white sharks mating. However, scientists have observed other shark species mating. Scientists believe great whites mate in a way similar to other sharks. Male sharks have tube-like organs called claspers. The two claspers extend from the male shark's pelvic fins. The male grabs the female with his teeth and inserts one of his claspers. He keeps her still during mating by biting her pectoral fin.

Dangerous Childhood

Scientists believe female great white sharks are pregnant for as long as 12 months. Mother sharks give birth in the spring and summer, when waters are warmer. A mother shark usually has between 2 and 14

Great white shark pups look very similar to adult great whites.

pups. Unlike most other fish, great white shark pups hatch inside their mother. Then they are born live.

The pups look like miniature adult sharks. They are already between 4 to 5 feet (1.2 to 1.5 m) long. They weigh approximately 26 to 33 pounds (12 to 15 kg). Once the mother shark gives birth, her job is finished. She swims away. The pups must survive on their own. Fortunately great white pups are equipped with sharp teeth. They are able to hunt right away.

Mechanical Monster

One of the world's most famous great white sharks was born on land. A famous great white shark starred in *Jaws*, a 1975 blockbuster movie. The film tells the story of a fictional killer shark that terrorizes swimmers off a New England island. *Jaws* was so terrifying that it kept many moviegoers out of ocean waters that summer. However, the shark in the film wasn't real. A top shark expert helped design the mechanical monster, nicknamed Bruce.

Growing pups eat a variety of fish. One of their favorites is tuna. Pups also eat rays, squid, and a variety of bottom fishes. Young great whites sometimes feed on smaller sharks. But pups have to be careful. They are targets for bigger ocean predators. Adult sharks and killer whales prowl the waters searching for tasty little pups to snack upon. Many pups don't reach their first birthday.

Growing Up

Great white pups grow approximately 1 foot (30 cm) per year. When they're full grown, great whites can be

The mechanical great white shark used in *Jaws* looked lifelike to moviegoers.

Once they are full grown, great whites are top predators. But not many great white sharks survive past their first few years.

as long as 21 feet (6.4 m). Females are usually bigger than males.

Males will usually weigh in at 1,500 to 2,200 pounds (680–1,000 kg). Females usually weigh between 2,200 and 4,200 pounds (1,000–1,900 kg). Gigantic great whites can weigh more than 5,000 pounds (2,300 kg).

Great white sharks that survive to adulthood usually live for 40 to 50 years. But the oldest great whites can reach 60 years of age or older. Although great white sharks are long-lived, their population is low. This is because they don't have babies very often compared to other fish, and many pups don't survive to adulthood.

FURTHER EVIDENCE

Chapter Two covers the life cycle of a great white shark. What was one of the chapter's main points? What are some pieces of evidence in the chapter that support this main point? Check out the Web site at the link below. Does the information on this Web site support the main point in this chapter? Write a few sentences using new information from the Web site as evidence to support the main point in this chapter.

Great White Shark Life Cycle
www.mycorelibrary.com/great-white-shark

CHAPTER THREE

PICKY PREDATORS

Great whites might be super hunters. But they are known for being picky eaters.

An adult great white feasts mostly on marine mammals whose blubber is high in fat. The shark's favorite foods include dolphins, elephant seals, sea lions, seals, and small whales. Strong jaws and sharp teeth are the shark's only weapons for catching a meal. The great white's jaws and teeth are strong

A great white leaps out of the water with a decoy seal in its mouth. Researchers use decoy seals to attract sharks.

With their high fat content, seals are some of great white sharks' favorite foods.

enough to crunch hard bones and slice through tough skin. After a gigantic meal, great whites don't need to eat again for up to two months!

Great whites use all their senses to search for supper. They sniff out a meal with sensitive, blood-detecting noses. Then they use their powerful tails and fins to swim toward their prey.

Surprise Attack

Once a great white senses tasty prey, the hunt is on. A shark usually patrols the bottom of the ocean. It patiently waits to spot a seal or sea lion swimming above. Then the great white zooms upward, launching a surprise attack. Its jaws snap down on the prey in a deadly grasp.

A great white sometimes shoots up toward its prey so fast that it launches into the air. This amazing leap is known as a breach. Then the shark splashes down with its prize clenched tightly in its powerful jaws.

The Wrong Taste

Each year, sharks attack an average of 100 humans around the world. Great white sharks are responsible for about one-third of these attacks. However, according to scientists, the curious creatures are most likely sample biting. From below, surfboards and wetsuits with fins look similar to seal silhouettes. But unlike seals, humans are made of tough muscles instead of fatty blubber. Great white sharks usually spit out their human victims after tasting them. A human has a greater chance of dying from a bolt of lightning or a bee sting than a great white shark attack.

Ancient Fish

Great white sharks' ancestors were around long before the dinosaurs roamed the earth. Modern great whites have many of the same predatory traits and behaviors as ancient sharks. Their prehistoric relatives appeared in seas 400 million years ago. A monster shark called the *megalodon*, also known as the giant megatooth, was as big and heavy as a railroad car. Its jaws stretched more than 6 feet (1.8 m) wide and 7 feet (2.1 m) high. Huge teeth chomped deep into the megalodon's prey, most likely whales. This massive shark was one of the biggest, most powerful predators in history.

Spy Hopping and Bumping

Great whites are one of the few sharks that raise their heads out of the water. They occasionally pop up to the surface to observe their environment and hopefully spot a meal. This behavior is known as spy hopping. Sharks will sometimes bump into prey before fully attacking. They use their special pores to identify animals.

What happens if two great whites have their eyes on the same seal for a meal? The first

A great white shark breaches.

A great white shark breaks the surface to check out an object floating in the water. Sharks often pop up to the surface, hoping to find food.

shark does a tail slap. The shark slaps the surface of the ocean with its tail. The movement shoots water toward the second shark. This behavior lets the second great white know who is the top shark.

STRAIGHT TO THE SOURCE

Getting attacked by a shark is extremely unlikely. In fact, according to the International Shark Attack File, there were only 75 incidents of unprovoked shark attack on humans worldwide in 2011. These attacks resulted in 12 deaths. Since divers spend more time in the water than other people, they are more likely to encounter sharks. This advice from the International Shark Attack File is geared toward divers:

> *If a shark actually gets you in its mouth, I advise to be as aggressively defensive as you are able. "Playing dead" does not work. Pound the shark in any way possible. Try to claw at the eyes and gill openings, two very sensitive areas. Once released, do all you can to exit the water as quickly as possible because with your blood in the water, the shark very well could return for a repeat attack.*

Source: George H. Burgess. "Shark Attacks: Advice to Divers Encountering a Shark." Ichthyology. *Florida Museum of Natural History, n.d. Web. Accessed January 18, 2013.*

What's the Big Idea?

Read this advice carefully. What is the author trying to say about how a diver should act during a shark attack? Pick out two details the author uses to make his point. Why isn't playing dead a good strategy?

CHAPTER FOUR

GREAT WHITES AT HOME

Like humans, great white sharks are warm-blooded. This means they raise their body temperature above the surrounding water temperature. The great white sharks' distribution ranges from the cool northern waters to the tropical equator. They also live in the more temperate Atlantic, Pacific, and Indian oceans.

Great white sharks can be found in ocean waters around the world.

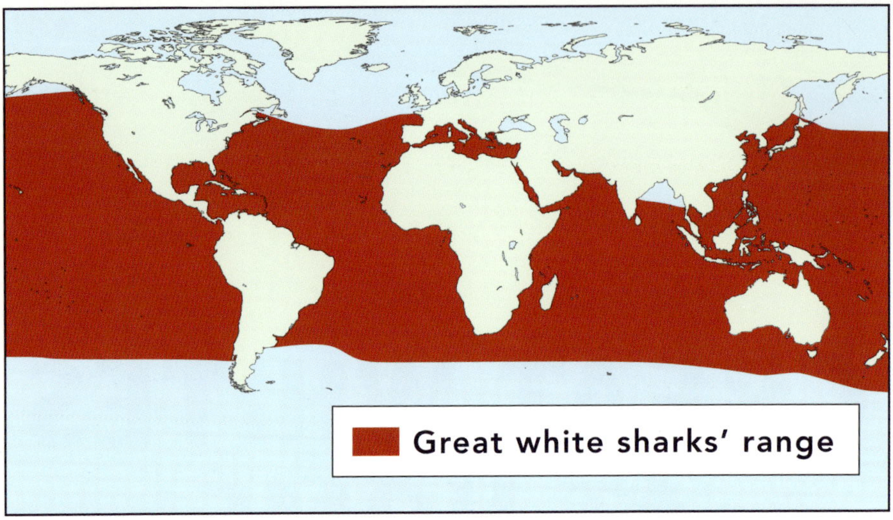

Huge Habitat

Look at the range map of all the different locations that great whites call home. Why would great whites choose to live in these areas? What characteristics make the sharks well adapted to these habitats? Write a short paragraph describing the great white shark's habitat.

Great whites have one of the widest ranges of any marine animal. These sharks spend most of their time along the coasts of Africa, North America, South America, Australia, China, Japan, Korea, the Mediterranean, and New Zealand. Most great whites congregate near big seal and sea lion colonies. That way they're always assured of a tasty meal!

Great white sharks migrate, or travel, long distances. They sometimes cross entire oceans in their quest for food. Scientists tracked one shark that made an amazing journey from South Africa to Australia. This is the longest recorded migration for any fish.

The White Shark Café

Great whites also make shorter migrations to eat, meet, and mate. In the United States, great whites migrate back and forth between the coastal California waters and the Hawaiian Islands. Midway on their journey, they stop at a spot scientists have nicknamed The White Shark Café.

This spot in the middle of the ocean isn't known for having a large

Shark Sleuths

How do scientists document great white sharks' migrations? They capture, tag, and release adult sharks. First, scientists use chum, or fish bait, to lure sharks next to a small boat. Then they hook the shark and load it onto a platform. Once the shark is on the boat, they measure and weigh the animal. They also take samples of its blood and tissue. Next, they attach a satellite tag to the shark's dorsal fin. The shark is released back in the water within 15 minutes.

Scientists tag a great white shark off the coast of Massachusetts before releasing it back into the ocean.

fish population. However, sharks often visit this spot in the spring and early summer. So scientists began to study the area. Males usually arrive at the café first. Once there, they begin diving again and again. Scientists now think the sharks are gobbling up giant squid. Females arrive in spring and early summer. But the café may be more than a squid buffet.

Many scientists believe most great whites mate in spring and early summer. This is also when the most great whites are visiting the White Shark Café. The café could also be a mating spot!

EXPLORE ONLINE

Chapter Four discusses how scientists track and study great white sharks. Whenever a shark's tagged fin breaks the surface, it signals a satellite. The signal is beamed back from space, allowing scientists to track the shark's location on an online map. Visit the Web site below to see the current locations of some great white sharks researchers are studying. How is the information in the Web site similar to the information in Chapter Four? How is it different?

Shark Tracker

www.mycorelibrary.com/great-white-shark

BE SHARK SMART
INFORMATION
• Great White Sharks naturally occur in these waters all year round
• Great White Sharks are predators, and are dangerous animals
• Encounters with sharks are rare, but please remain alert
• Great White Sharks are known to use the inshore area
• Great White Sharks are an important part of the natural marine environment
INLIGTING
• Witdoodhaaie kom regdeur die jaar natuurlik in hierdie water voor
• Witdoodhaaie is roofvisse en dus gevaarlik
• Haaivoorvalle is skaars maar wees asseblief versigtig
• Witdoodhaaie kom van tyd tot tyd naby die kus voor
• Witdoodhaaie vorm 'n belangrike deel van die natuurlike see-omgewing
INGCACISO
• Kukho ooKrebe abaKhulu abaMhlophe kule ndawo unyaka wonke
• OoKrebe abaKhulu abaMhlophe ngawona marhamncwa aqwengayo yaye zizilwanyana eziyingozi
• Anqabile amathuba okudibana nooKrebe kodwa ncedani nihlale nilumkile
• OoKrebe abaKhulu abaMhlophe bayaziwa ngokuthanda ukudada kwindawo ekufuphi nonxweme
• OoKrebe abaKhulu abaMhlophe bayinxalenye ebalulekileyo kwimeko-bume esingqongileyo yendalo yaselwandle
SAFETY TIPS
DO
• Swim, surf, surfski, or kayak in groups
• Swim close to shore / in waist deep water
• Consider using a personal shark shield for surfing or kayaking
VEILIGHEIDSWENKE
MOETS
• Swem, branderplankry, branderski of kajakroei in groepe
• Swem naby aan die kus of in middellyf-diep water
• Oorweeg dit om 'n persoonlike haaiskild te gebruik wanneer jy kajakroei of branderplankry
INGCEBISO ZOKHUSELEKO
OMA UKWENZE
• Dadani, nityibilize ngamaplanga, okanye ngekayak ningamaqela
• Dadelani kufuphi nonxweme / emanzini ama esinqeni
• Kungaluncedo ukusebenzisa ikhakha lokuzikhusela kookrebe

CHAPTER FIVE

A PREDATOR IN JEOPARDY

Adult great white sharks are some of the toughest fish in the ocean. It might not seem like great whites would need to worry about predators. However, these fierce fish are food for other ocean creatures, especially orcas, or killer whales.

Great whites' most dangerous predator actually comes from land. Humans around the world fear

Many humans fear great white sharks. However, humans put great white sharks in greater danger than any other predator.

sharks. In fact, sharks have more reason to fear humans.

Getting Up Close and Personal with Great Whites

Shark-cage diving is catching on with wildlife tourists. These shark fans face great white sharks with nothing between them but thick aluminum bars. First the person puts on a wetsuit and mask. Then the person enters a deep-sea cage and drops down 30 feet (9 m) into the ocean. The person uses a special breathing system to draw in air. From the cage, great white sharks can be observed in their natural habitat. The cage-diving industry lets people get to know sharks better. This is helping protect sharks around the world.

Human Hunters

In the United States and many other countries, it is illegal to keep great white sharks after catching them. It is illegal to sell shark parts in many places. But other countries permit people to fish for sharks commercially, or to sell.

When sharks become human prey, people use them for many different products. Shark meat is sliced into fillets for food. Shark liver oil is turned

A diver gets ready to come face to face with a shark off the coast of Guadalupe Island, Mexico.

into lubricants, cosmetics, and fuel. Shark cartilage is used in health supplements. Sharkskin is made into exotic leather. Other shark parts, such as teeth and jawbones, are sold as trophies.

The most valuable part of a shark is its fin. In some Asian countries, shark-fin soup is considered a delicacy. Some sharks are hunted solely for their fins.

The dorsal fin is the most valuable part of a great white shark. Some people believe shark fins have many health benefits, including helping prevent heart disease.

In a practice known as finning, fishers slice fins off great whites. Then the fishers toss the still-living shark into the sea. Great whites need their fins to swim, so they are doomed to die without them.

Saving Sharks

Today many conservation groups are fighting to list the great white shark under the US Endangered

Species Act. Sharks prevent populations of prey species from growing too high. A reduction in great white sharks can have a ripple effect. This could throw entire ecosystems out of balance.

It's difficult to keep great whites in captivity. However, Project White Shark at California's Monterey Bay Aquarium has exhibited six sharks. Eventually, the sharks are returned to the wild. Millions of visitors came face-to-face with the six sharks. After seeing great whites up close, many people's ideas about sharks change. They're encouraged to conserve great whites.

Unlikely Supporters

A group of shark-attack survivors has come together to save the very creatures that attacked them. A survivor who works for an environmental organization organized the group. Its members speak out against the sale of shark fins for soup. They also hope to raise awareness about the important role sharks play in the environment. They want to draw attention to the world's declining shark population.

Visitors see great white sharks up close at the Monterey Bay Aquarium.

Great white sharks are important predators. They have been around for millions of years. It's up to us to protect these amazing creatures and keep them swimming in the world's oceans.

STRAIGHT TO THE SOURCE

In 2012 Australia announced a plan to kill sharks swimming near beaches. The plan will also target the great white shark. The Sea Shepherd Conservation Society spoke out against Australia's plan:

> *The world cannot afford to lose any more sharks. Like them or not, we need sharks on this planet. As apex predators, they keep our oceans healthy. Sharks are a critical component in an ecosystem that controls our planet's temperature and weather, provides one-third of the world with food, and generates more oxygen than all the rainforests combined. Recent studies indicate that regional elimination of sharks has caused disastrous effects including the collapse of fisheries and the death of coral reefs. Kill the sharks and Australia's healthy, beautiful coastline will join countless other ocean dead zones.*

Source: Julie Andersen. "Sea Shepherd Cries Foul Over Western Australia Shark Cull." October 1, 2012. Sea Shepherd. *Sea Shepherd Conservation Society, 2013. Web. Accessed January 18, 2013.*

Back It Up

The author of this passage is using evidence to support her opinion. Write a paragraph describing the author's point of view. Then write down two or three pieces of evidence the author uses to make her point.

FAST FACTS

Common Name: Great white shark

Scientific Name: *Carcharodon carcharias*

Average Size: 13 to 20 feet (4–6 m)

Average Weight: Males usually weigh between 1,500 and 2,200 pounds (680–1,000 kg); females usually weigh between 2,200 and 4,200 pounds (1,000–1,900 kg)

Color: Dark gray back with white underbelly

Average Lifespan: 40 to 50 years

Diet: Mostly marine mammals, such as dolphins, elephant seals, sea lions, seals, and small whales, with occasional sea birds and other sharks; young great whites eat fish, rays, and other sharks

Habitat: Cool ocean waters worldwide

Predators: Orcas and humans

Did You Know?

- Females give birth to between two and ten shark pups at a time.
- Great whites swim as fast as 35 miles per hour (56 km/h).
- A great white shark has approximately 300 teeth.

STOP AND THINK

Take a Stand

This book discusses how sharks are prized for their fins. Do you think shark-fin soup should be banned from menus? Or should restaurants continue to serve this soup? Write a letter explaining your opinion. Be sure to back up your viewpoint with reasons that are supported by facts.

You Are There

This book discusses how some survivors of shark attacks are sticking up for the very creatures that attacked them. Imagine that a great white bit your foot. At first you might have been angry. Then you read about how other survivors formed a group to speak up for sharks. Would you be tempted to join this group? How do you think your personal story would help others understand sharks better and learn to respect them?

Say What?

Learning about great white sharks can mean learning a lot of new vocabulary. Search for five words in this book that you've never seen or heard before. Then look up their meanings in a dictionary. Finally, use each word in a sentence about great white sharks.

Why Do I Care?

Great white sharks are tricky creatures to keep in captivity. Why would you buy a ticket to view a great white? How do you think your opinion of predators would change after watching a shark eat a meal?

GLOSSARY

blubber
fat of large marine mammals

camouflage
patterns or coloring that help disguise or hide an animal

cartilage
elastic tissue that forms the skeleton of sharks

ecosystem
the group of plants and animals living in and interacting with their environment

migrate
to move from one region or climate to another for breeding or feeding

pups
young sharks

serrated
with notches like the teeth of a saw

temperate
a climate that is moderate or mild in temperature

warm-blooded
able to regulate body temperature without an outside source

LEARN MORE

Books

Civard-Racinais, Alexandrine. *The Great White Shark: Myth and Reality.* Buffalo, New York: Firefly Books, 2012.

MacQuitty, Miranda. *Eyewitness Shark.* New York: DK Publishing, 2008.

Mathea, Heidi. *Great White Sharks.* Edina, MN: ABDO, 2011.

Web Links

To learn more about great white sharks, visit ABDO Publishing Company online at **www.abdopublishing.com**. Web sites about great white sharks are featured on our Book Links page. These links are routinely monitored and updated to provide the most current information available.

Visit **www.mycorelibrary.com** for free additional tools for teachers and students.

INDEX

ABOUT THE AUTHOR

Nancy Furstinger is the author of nearly 100 books. She has been a feature writer for a daily newspaper, a managing editor of trade and consumer magazines, and an editor at two children's book publishing houses.